THIS BOOK BELONGS TO

.... Jacqui ....

An ANNABEL LANGBEIN BOOK

First published in 2008 by Annabel Langbein Books.

An imprint of The International Culinary Institute Press Ltd.

PO Box 99068 Newmarket, Auckland, New Zealand

ISBN 978-0-9582029-6-1

Design Donna Cross, Three Eyes Ltd

Copy Editors Mia Yardley, Jane Turner

Production ICIP

Printed in China

www.annabel-langbein.com

CELEBRATE

A Calendar of Cakes for Special Dates

BY ANNABEL LANGBEIN

ILLUSTRATIONS ANNIE HAYWARD

annabel langbein books

INTRODUCTION

It's a great thing tradition. Without it, what pattern would mark the important ceremonies and events in our lives? Annual rituals of celebration give us surety and add rhythm to our days, ever more vital as the world whirls madly by.

Throughout the year, special dates see us gather together in collective celebrations of culture and religion. Then there are the special personal occasions within families and amongst friends – birthdays, weddings and special achievements, all of which deserve to be remembered and celebrated.

When I was a child, my mother kept a well-worn Winnie the Pooh birthday book near the phone. In it she listed important dates – birthdays of friends and family, anniversaries and other special celebrations. All were noted and as a result, never forgotten.

I hope that this book will be something you enjoy and treasure for decades, creating an heirloom to pass down through the generations. In the remembrance of family traditions, we create our own special histories and give pattern to our lives. What form will your memories take?

It has been my greatest pleasure to work with Annie Hayward who created the charming and whimsical illustrations in this book. Her work captures the pleasures and joy of life. Many thanks also to Donna Cross who designed this book, making it as useful as it is beautiful.

Thank you both for such a lovely project to work on.

Annabel

2008

January

The Hesperides

Gaia, the Mother Earth, created the first apple tree for the wedding of the goddess Hera to Zeus. It bore golden fruit of such beauty Hera planted the tree in the Garden of the Hesperides on the slopes of Mount Atlas and entrusted its guardianship to the three nymphs born of the evening star, Hesperus. As daughters of the evening, the Hesperides were regarded as the source of the radiant light at sunset. They were wondrous singers and in keeping with their custody of Gaia's wedding gift they heralded the marriages of many heroes with joyful song. As the birth of new beginnings, the ancients thought of January as the month of marriages.

GARNET

The word garnet is derived from
granatus, the Latin for grain or seed,
thanks to its similarity to a pomegranate
seed. January's birthstone has long been
a talisman for the traveller, offering
protection from evil and disaster.
It is said that Noah hung a lantern of
garnets in the ark to shed light during
the dark nights of the flood.

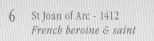

JANUARY

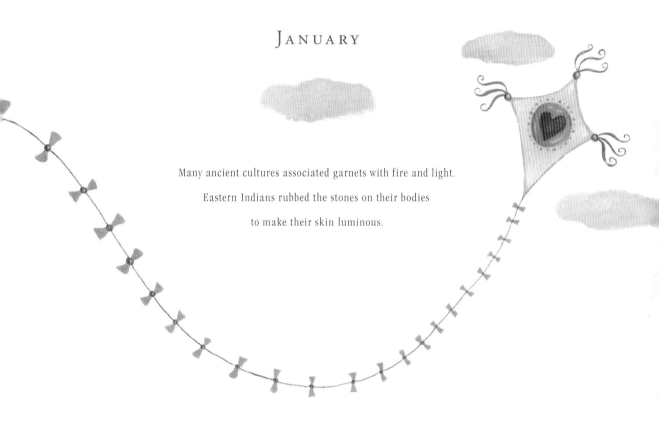

Many ancient cultures associated garnets with fire and light.

Eastern Indians rubbed the stones on their bodies

to make their skin luminous.

17	18
19	20
21	22
23	24

CAPRICORN - *Dec 22 - Jan 19*

When the monster Typhon, enemy of Zeus,
appeared in Egypt to threaten the great
Greek gods, Pan, god of shepherds and flocks,
hunting and rustic music, warned his fellow
deities and bade them transform themselves
into wild beasts to deceive the monster. In
appreciation, Zeus ordained that
Pan's likeness be set amongst the
constellations as the goat-fish
Aeocerus, the stars we now
call Capricorn.

JANUARY

Those born under Capricorn
are said to possess vision and
ambition. By nature, they are
responsible, focused and dependable.
They respect loyalty and commitment,
but while they abhor indecisiveness
they refuse to be bossed.

25

26

27

Wolfgang Amadeus
Mozart - 1756
Austrian composer

28

29

30

31

Carnation

JANUARY

CHOCOLATE, FOOD OF THE GODS

The tropical cacao tree, Theobroma cacao, is the source of chocolate, a food unrivalled for the pleasure it has bestowed on mankind. The Greek word theobroma literally means "food of the gods". Cacao has been cultivated for more than two thousand years. The Aztecs used it as trading currency (100 cacao beans could buy a slave). They also believed chocolate conferred wisdom and vitality. It was reserved for warriors, priests and the nobility who consumed it as a hot, frothy beverage. In the modern world, the stimulant and restorative properties of chocolate are still appreciated, but for most of us, chocolate is simply the most delicious treat.

MISSISSIPPI MUD CAKE WITH CHOCOLATE GANACHE, *recipe page 102*

VIOLETS FOR IO

Violets were one of the favourite flowers of the Ancient Greeks. When Zeus seduced the nymph Io, he transformed her into a beautiful heifer to deceive his wife, the goddess Hera. In her new form, Io was forced to eat grass. As she wept over its bitter taste and coarse texture, Zeus transformed her tears into dainty, sweet-smelling flowers and bade her to eat the blossoms we now know as violets.

AQUARIUS - *Jan 20 - Feb 18*

Ganymede, a young prince of

    Troy and the most handsome of mortals,

was abducted by Zeus to serve as his cupbearer.

    From Olympus, Ganymede saw that the people on earth

had a great need for water and pleaded successfully with Zeus to send rain.

      He was glorified as Aquarius, god of rain, and placed amongst the stars.

FEBRUARY

Like their namesake, Aquarians are
natural humanitarians with an
independent spirit. Charming and kind, they
make friends easily and are always ready
to listen to those in need.

There is no

small pleasure

in sweet water.

OVID

17	18
19	20
21	22
23	24

23
Samuel Pepys - 1633
English diarist

FEBRUARY

AMETHYST

The Greek word amethystos translates as "not intoxicated".
The stone was believed to keep its wearer from becoming drunk;
thus wine goblets were often carved from amethyst. Amethysts
represent stability, insight and sincerity. In Tibet, the gem
is considered sacred to Buddha and is regarded as a
symbol of peace. Wearing amethysts is thought to
ease the pain of grief and promote happiness,
satisfaction and good fortune.

25

26

27

28

29

Violet

FEBRUARY

CHERRIES FROM THE OLD WORLD

That most beautiful fruit, the red, heart-shaped cherry, has been treasured in Asia and Europe for centuries. Archaeologists have discovered cherry stones at many dig sites, proving that wild cherries were eaten in Bronze Age Europe and Ancient China. The Greeks brought the cultivated cherry from Persia and the Romans ensured that the fruit was cultivated throughout Europe. Hundreds of varieties now exist but all originate from two wild species: the sweet and the sour. The sweet cherry is eaten fresh; the sour is used for preserving and cooking.

CATHEDRAL CAKE, *recipe page 104*

DIONYSUS, GOD OF WINE

For more than two millennia, festivals were held in Ancient Greece and Rome to

celebrate the coming of spring and the maturing of

the previous year's vintage. Processions of garlanded men

and women revelled in games and contests

of music and poetry, all paying homage to Dionysus,

the son of Zeus, also known as Bacchus. As the god of wine and festivities and the

patron deity of the theatre, his name is still a byword for intoxicating pleasures.

1 2 3 4

PISCES - *Feb 19 - Mar 20*

Aphrodite, the goddess of love,
pleasure and joy, was born of the
sea and rose fully-grown from the
waves on a seashell.
She was accompanied to the shore
by a retinue, which included two
sea-centaurs, Bythos and Aphros,
otherwise known as
Sea-Depths and Sea-Foam.

9 10 11 12

Mrs Isabella Beaton - 1836
English cookbook author

March

Pisceans are peaceable,
sensitive, poetic and modest.
They are good-natured but they
sometimes need guidance. Once
set on their own paths they are
loath to deny them.

17	18
19	20
21	22
23	24 Harry Houdini - 1874 *American escapologist*

AQUAMARINE

Aquamarine comes from the Latin aqua marina,
meaning "water of the sea". The stone is said to be
a particularly strong talisman when immersed
in water. Legends say that aquamarine is
mermaids' treasure with the power to keep
sailors safe. Those going to sea would put
the stones under their pillows to
ensure calm waters
and a safe voyage.

MARCH

With a blue glow reminiscent of calm seas and
cloudless skies, aquamarine has a soothing
effect on its wearer and on relationships.
In the Middle Ages, it was believed that
aquamarine could cure the effects of
poison and help couples to work out their
differences and build a strong, happy marriage.

25

26

27

28

29

30

31

Daffodil

MEDIEVAL MARZIPAN

The treat we know as Marzipan is believed to have originated in the Middle East

and was introduced to Europe in the late Middle Ages.

Made from sugar and ground almonds

(with a few bitter almonds added for flavour), marzipan has

always been known for its sculptural properties.

Medieval feasts were punctuated by the presentation of marzipan

figurines, often allegorical, to be admired and then consumed.

Today, Sicily remains one of the best places to find realistic

miniatures of vegetables, fruit and animals moulded in marzipan.

EASTER SIMNEL CAKE, *recipe page 106*

The Gods of Wind

The Anemoi, the Greek gods of wind,

each personified a directional and

seasonal power. From the north

came the cold, wintry breath of Boreas.

His counterpart was the hot southerly wind, Notus,

who sent rainstorms during late summer and autumn.

In the east unlucky Eurus prevailed

and from the west Zephyr sent sweet, fruitful

breezes to herald the beginning of

spring and summer.

APRIL

DIAMONDS

The Greeks believed
diamonds were the
tears of the gods; in
Roman mythology they were
splinters from fallen stars. During the
Middle Ages it was believed that
diamonds would grow dark in
the face of guilt and shine brightly for
the innocent. Today diamonds
symbolize eternity and love.

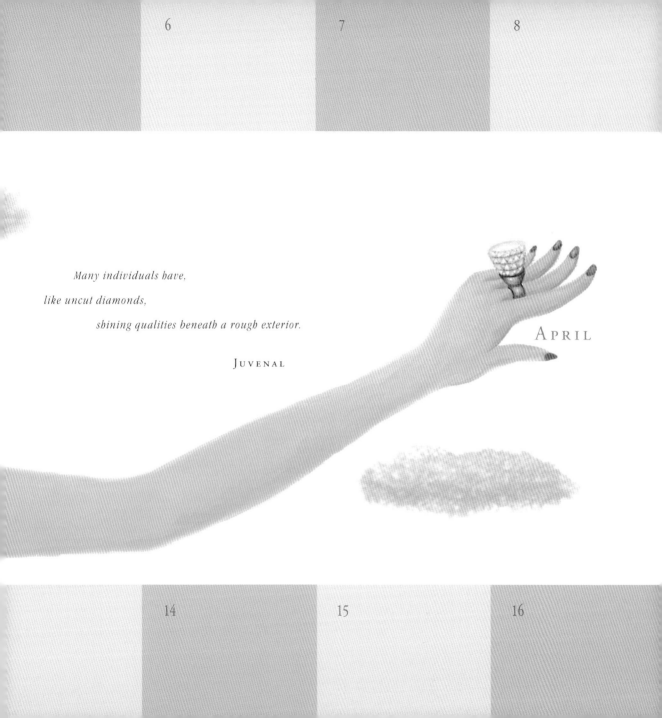

Many individuals have,

like uncut diamonds,

shining qualities beneath a rough exterior.

JUVENAL

APRIL

17	18
19	20
21	22
23	24

23
William Shakespeare
- 1564
*English playwright
& poet*

The Ancient Babylonian calendar represented Aries
as a labourer; later the star sign became
known as the ram. According to Greek
legend, Alectryon was a youth who
was ordered by Ares, the god
of war, to stand guard
outside his door while
he conducted
an illicit dalliance
with Aphrodite.

ARIES - *Mar 21 - Apr 19*

However, the young man fell asleep
and Helios, the sun god, discovered the couple.
Ares turned Alectryon into a rooster, destined to announce the
approach of the sun every morning.
Arians are defined by an open and enthusiastic nature.
They can be outspoken and quick to act, yet being
amiable, rarely cause offence.

APRIL

25	26
27	28
29	30

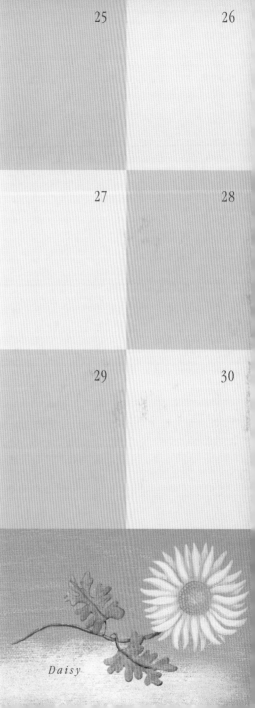

Daisy

SUN-KISSED APRICOTS

This velvet-skinned, fragrant
stone fruit is native to
China. Introduced to Persia
and Armenia via the silk trade
routes around the 1st century BC,
apricots became integral to Middle Eastern
culture and cuisine, where they are still enjoyed
in both savoury and dessert dishes. The apricot
has a short life; lucky are those who can eat a
ripe apricot straight from the tree, where
its sun-kissed flavour remains unrivalled, but
happily it is also the perfect dried fruit.

APRICOT & ALMOND LAYERED WEDDING CAKE
WITH WHITE CHOCOLATE ICING, *recipe page 108*

APRIL,

CANDLES FOR ARTEMIS

The birthdays of Greek deities were celebrated each month and therefore

each god was honoured with twelve different fêtes a year.

The birthday of Artemis, goddess of the moon and the hunt,

was celebrated on the sixth day of the month.

Worshippers made a large round cake with flour and honey, representing

the full moon. Candles were lit on the cake as a

symbol of moonlight, the goddess's

earthward radiance.

MAY

EMERALDS

This green gem has been mined from the depths of the earth for over four thousand years. In Babylonian times emeralds represented love and fertility, while the Ancient Romans believed in its healing powers. Emeralds are also associated with a keen intelligence and powers of divination – giving credence to the belief that those who wear emeralds are guaranteed a happy and successful life.

Florence Nightingale - 182C
*English pioneer of
modern nursing*

6   7   8

MAY

Emeralds, alone of precious stones,

    satisfy our gaze without causing a surfeit of colour...

So soothing is the mellow green of the gem for tired eyes.

PLINY THE ELDER

14   15   16

17	18
19 Malcolm X - 1925 *American civil rights* *activist*	20
21	22
23	24

TAURUS *- April 20 - May 20*

Zeus, king of the Greek gods, disguised himself as a
bull to win the heart of the Phoenician princess,
Europa. He bound off with her across the
seas to a new land he called Europe. Those born
under the constellation of Taurus are steady,
loving people with a determined
streak. Taureans enjoy the good
things in life and are house-proud.

The gods themselves,

> *Humbling their deities to love, have taken*
> *The shapes of beasts upon them, Jupiter*
> > *Became a bull, and bellow'd.*

SHAKESPEARE

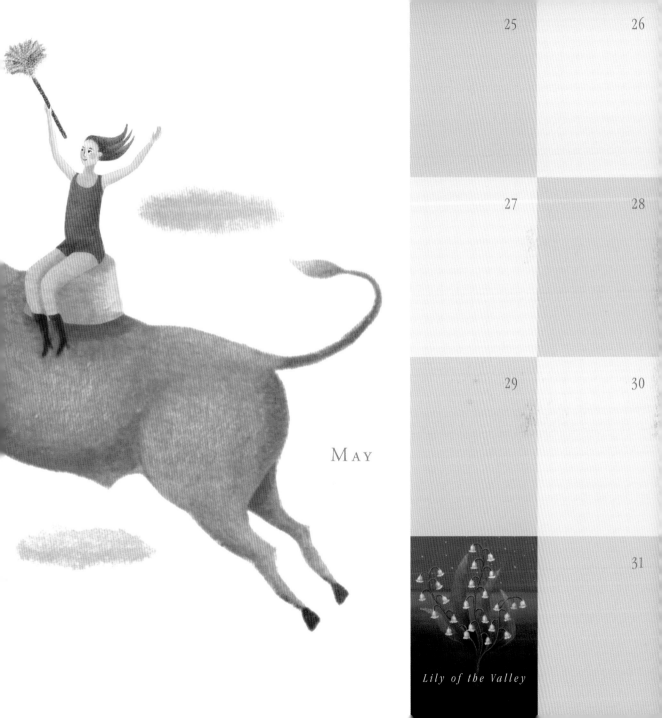

25

26

27

28

MAY

29

30

31

Lily of the Valley

Ice Cream Pleasures

The origins of today's ice cream reaches as far back as the 4th century BC

when Alexander the Great favoured frozen wine.

In 62 AD the Roman emperor Nero despatched slaves to the mountains

to collect snow and ice, which was flavoured

with nectar, fruit pulp and honey to create sorbet.

By the sixteenth century the Italians had developed an academy

devoted to the study of ice and ice cream making.

White Chocolate & Raspberry Bombe Alaska, *recipe page 110*

May

BELWE, THE SUN BEARER

Belwe, the sun goddess of the Sami, the indigenous people

of the Arctic, travelled the sky with her daughter Belwe-Neida

in a carriage made of antlers, bringing spring to a land

enveloped in cold and darkness. When she appeared,

the Sami smothered their bodies in butter so that

Belwe could absorb the rich food and recharge

her light beams for the long journey

back across the sky.

 JUNE

PEARL

The early Chinese told of pearls falling from the
sky when dragons fought, while in Ancient India
it was believed that they were created from early
morning dewdrops. Romans conjectured that the water
that spilled from Venus' body as she rose out of
the sea was so affected by her beauty that
the drops changed into pearls.

Anne Frank - 1929
*Jewish Dutch World War I
diarist*

The rarest things in the world,
next to a spirit of discernment, are
diamonds and pearls.

JEAN DE LA BRUYÈRE

JUNE

17	18
19	20
21 Jean-Paul Sartre - 1905 *French philosopher*	22
23	24

GEMINI - *May 21 - Jun 21*

Usually represented by the twins Castor and Pollux,
Gemini symbolizes the duality of reason and
emotion, or civilization and nature.

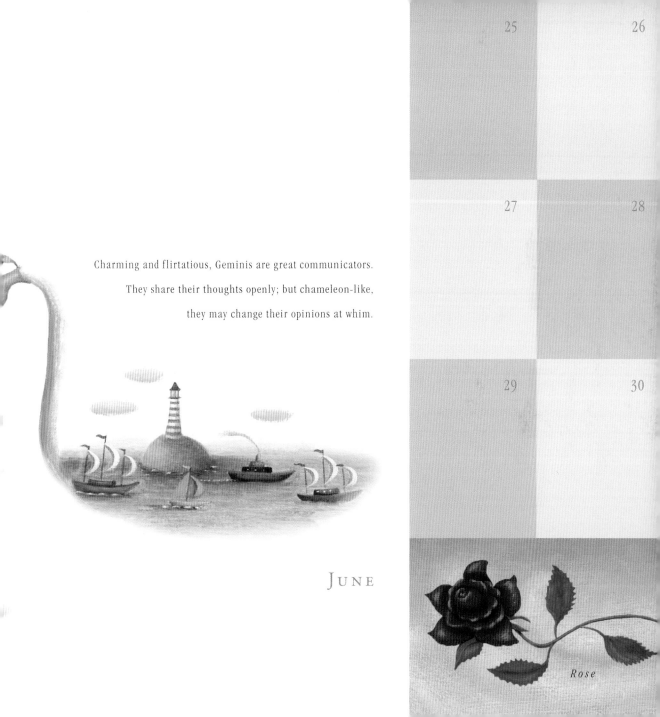

Charming and flirtatious, Geminis are great communicators.
They share their thoughts openly; but chameleon-like,
they may change their opinions at whim.

25	26
27	28
29	30

JUNE

Rose

Soothing Vanilla

Vanilla, a sweet, aromatic spice, is derived from the cured pod of
the tropical orchid Vanilla planifolia. The Totonac people of Mexico
first cultivated vanilla. They sent vanilla as tribute payment to their
conquerors, the Aztecs. In turn, the invading Spanish took the spice
back to Europe as booty. The Spanish word vainilla means "little pod".
Vanilla is a soothing spice; a drop of vanilla added to warm
milk will settle a fractious child.

LEMON & VANILLA BUTTERFLY CUPCAKES, *recipe page 112*

JUNE

The Birth of Venus

Aphrodite, or Venus as the Romans knew her,

was the goddess of beauty, love and marriage. She was born fully-grown

from the foam of the sea.

At her first steps on land, flowers bloomed beneath her feet.

The pomegranate was sacred to Aphrodite, symbolizing female fertility

and the consummation of marriage.

Seeking her favour, Roman brides wore pomegranate-twig wreaths,

although the goddess herself

was an inconstant wife.

July

CANCER - *Jun 22 - Jul 22*

In Ancient Greek astrology, Hermes ruled the sign of Cancer,
which was deemed a musical sign. On adding strings to a tortoise
shell, Hermes invented the lyre. Hermes was the god of
many contrary aspects of life – from travel,
hospitality and diplomacy to thievery,
language and cunning.

Cancerians are known to be similarly variable; they can easily transform from being shy and withdrawn to brilliant and friendly. At their core they are kind, conscientious and domestic.

JULY

17

18
Nelson Mandela - 1918
South African
anti-apartheid activist
& former President

19

20

21

22

23

24

RUBY

Prized by kings throughout the ages, rubies were thought to confer
health, wealth, wisdom and success upon their wearers.
Historically, the ruby has been symbolic of love and passion,
considered an aid to firm friendship and believed to ensure beauty.
Wearing rubies is said to banish sadness, while dreaming
of rubies augurs success and love.

The countless gold of a merry heart,
The rubies and pearls of a loving eye,
The indolent never can bring to the mart,
Nor the secret hoard up in his treasury.

WILLIAM BLAKE

JULY

25

26

27

28

29

30

31

Water Lily

GINGER TO HEAL

Ginger is a wonderfully piquant, fragrant spice obtained

from the fleshy stem root of the ginger plant.

Ginger originated in South East Asia

and remains integral to Asian cooking and medicine, where it is believed

to cleanse the blood, relieve unsettled stomachs and cure colds.

In the West, it has been prized since antiquity;

in Medieval Europe it was as common as pepper and used in all types of dishes.

In modern Western cooking ginger is often used as a dried spice in biscuits and cakes where it

adds a pleasant heat and a refreshing flavour.

GINGER CAKE WITH CARAMEL ICING, *recipe page 114.*

JULY

THE IMMORTAL HSI WANG MU

In Chinese legend Hsi Wang Mu, the Queen Mother of the West, was the personification of the feminine yin and the goddess of immortality. She lived in a golden palace in the Kunlun Mountains. Once every three thousand years, when the fruit of her sacred peach tree finally ripened, she threw a birthday party. On this special occasion the gods ate the peaches to renew their immortality.

AUGUST

Ancient Egyptians
believed that the world
was created when the sun was
in Leo.
Their astrologers
attributed the sign to the
lion-headed Sekhmet,
the terrifying aspect of
Hathor, goddess of
joy and love.

AUGUST

Leo - *Jul 23 - Aug 22*

As protector of both the living and the dead, Hathor was transformed into the murderous Sekhmet by the sun god Ra and unleashed against a rebellious mankind. As a fire sign, Leos are prone to dominate. They are capable of great generosity and warmth but can also be overbearing and judgemental. However, they are very loyal and fiercely protective of their loved ones.

14　　　　15　Napoleon Bonaparte - 1769　16
　　　　　　French Emperor

17	18
19	20
21	22
23	24

PERIDOT

Ancient Egyptians called this olive-green stone "the
gem of the sun". Curiously, crystals of peridot have
been found in fallen meteorites. The French word
peridot is derived from the Arabic faridat,
meaning gem. Peridot has been mined
for more than three thousand years; the
earliest deposits were discovered on
St. John's Island in the Red Sea. During the
Middle Ages, peridot was often used to decorate
European churches, perhaps because it was
believed the gem had the power to dissolve
enchantments and forestall evil.

AUGUST

25

26
Mother Theresa
– 1910
*Albanian nun &
missionary*

27

28

29

30

31

Poppy

FRAGRANT ORANGES

The oranges we eat today originated in China where they were valued for
fragrance as much as flavour. Early Chinese writings recommend
holding an orange in the hand to warm the fruit and release its perfume. While
the East enjoyed sweet oranges for hundreds of years, they did not reach Europe
until the late fifteenth century. Oranges were still a delicacy
and a sign of wealth well into modern times, and were placed as a treat in
children's Christmas stockings.

GREEK CITRUS CAKE, *recipe page 116*

AUGUST

Chih Nü and the Milky Way

Chih Nü, daughter of the Jade Emperor, the monarch of heaven,

was responsible for weaving clouds in the sky. She fell in love with a lowly

cowherd and neglected her duties. As punishment, her father transformed

the couple into the stars Vega and Altair, dividing them with a river,

the Milky Way. Out of pity, he allows the lovers to meet once a year. On the

seventh night of the seventh moon, he calls all the world's magpies

to build a bridge to reunite Chih Nü and her husband.

September

SEPTEMBER

1
2
3
4

9
10
11
12

Sapphires

Sapphires are known as the celestial gemstones, stemming
from the ancient Persian belief that the earth rested on a giant sapphire,
its reflection colouring the sky. The gem was originally
worn as a symbol of wisdom and purity; this is surely why
medieval kings wore sapphires to protect themselves from poison.
For many cultures, sapphires symbolized truth,
sincerity and fidelity, making the gem particularly appropriate
for lovers – in ancient times it was believed that the stone would
dim if the wearer had been unfaithful.

17

18

19

20

21

22

SEPTEMBER

23

24

VIRGO - *Aug 23 - Sep 22*

To the Ancient Greeks, she was Persephone,
abducted by Hades, god of the underworld, only
permitted to return to her mother, Demeter,
goddess of the earth, for half the year.
Virgo disappears from the skies each
autumn, and winter takes hold as
Demeter mourns her beloved daughter.
Virgos are earthy, practical and discriminating.
Known for their wit and wisdom, they often save the
day with their ability to unravel problems.

Not on one strand
are all life's jewels strung.

WILLIAM MORRIS

25

26

27

28

29

30

Rumi - 1207 AD
Persian poet

Aster

TROPICAL COCONUT

Coconut is abundant throughout the tropics. Its hard shell contains sweet juice and rich white flesh, which thickens and hardens as the fruit ripens. In Tahitian folklore, princess Hina was promised in marriage to the eel king, Te Tuna. Her brother Maui rescued the unwilling Hina by cutting off the eel's head, instructing his sister to bury it. She forgot and the head grew into a slender tree bearing fruit with a face – two eyes and a mouth, the coconut.

HUMMINGBIRD CAKE, *recipe page 118*

SEPTEMBER

October

Cleopatra's Triumph

Cleopatra VII, the last pharaoh of Ancient Egypt, was born in Alexandria in 69 B.C. She was famous for her sharp intelligence, charisma and seductive charms. When summoned to meet Mark Anthony she arrived in a magnificent barge with gilded stern and sails of purple. Dressed as Venus amidst dancing girls, musicians and attendants, she captivated Anthony with her splendour. Later she threw an immense celebration for his birthday and lavished the guests with gifts.

1

2

Mahatma Gandhi - 1869
Indian independence leader

3

4

October's child is born for woe,

And life's vicissitudes must know;

But lay on Opal on her breast,

And hope will lull those woes to rest.

ANONYMOUS

OCTOBER

9

10

11

12

OPAL

Among the ancients, rainbow-toned opals were a
symbol of fidelity. They were so favoured by the Romans that when
Mark Antony tried to buy Cleopatra a much-prized stone
the owner fled rather than give it up.
In the Middle Ages opals were believed to strengthen the eye
and, when worn as an amulet, gave the wearer
immunity from disease. Blonde women even wore
opal necklaces to protect the
colour of their hair.

17

18

19

20

21

22

23

24

OCTOBER

LIBRA - *Sep 23 - Oct 22*

Through the ages, Libra has represented
many forms of balance – between
esoteric and exoteric knowledge, summer and winter
and, rising as it does on the equinox,
between night and day.

Librans by nature
are sociable, charming and romantic.
They are idealistic, sometimes indecisive,
but always fair and balanced.

25

Pablo Picasso - 1881
Spanish artist

26

27

28

29

30

31

Calendula

OCTOBER

SUCCULENT RASPBERRIES

These rich, perfumed berries are very fragile and spoil easily.

Their sweet fruity acidity makes them suitable

for use in jams and sauces.

While they grow in several colours,

red berries are the most common.

According to Greek myth, all raspberries were white

until the god Jupiter, while still a child, threw a tantrum

and the nymph Ida tried to calm him with raspberries.

Collecting the berries, she pricked her finger on the thorns; her

blood stained the raspberries red forevermore.

ANGEL RASPBERRY LAYER CAKE, *recipe page 120*

November

Diwali, Festival of Light

Diwali, the festival of lights, marks the lunar New Year in the Hindu calendar and celebrates the triumph of goodness, light and knowledge over evil, darkness and ignorance. Celebrations last for five days, during which time buildings are adorned with oil lamps, homes are cleaned, windows opened and images of lotus flowers drawn to welcome Lakshmi, the Hindu goddess of wealth and good fortune. Lakshmi is usually depicted as a beautiful golden figure seated on a lotus flower, the Hindu symbol of purity and spiritual power.

1   2   3   4

November

Scorpios are courageous, adventurous and proud.
They may appear placid but you can
always count on a Scorpio for
deeply felt passions.

9   10   11   12

SCORPIO - *Oct 23 - Nov 21*

In Marshall Islands folklore, the sons of Ligedaner, Mother of the Stars,
competed in a sailing race for the title of King of the Heavens.
Ligedaner asked each to let her accompany them
but because of her heavy bags all but the youngest, Pleiades, refused.
Pleiades was rewarded - his mother carried new
sail rigging and he sped to the lead.
Dümur, the oldest son, tried to usurp the superior boat
but Ligedaner forced him to mount a sail on his own shoulders,
bending his back. Dümor lost the race
and his bent back can be seen in the curve
of the constellation Scorpio.

17	18
19	20
21	22
23	24

NOVEMBER

25	26
27	28
29	30

Jonathon Swift - 1667
Irish author & satirist

TOPAZ

Sanskrit for fire, topaz has long been associated
with warmth and passion. Ancient Egyptians believed
the golden hue of the jewel came from the light of the sun god Ra.
Hindus used topaz to protect their homes from
household fires. The stone is also a symbol of generosity and delight;
no wonder legend has it that topaz attracts
love to the wearer.

Chrysanthemum

NOVEMBER

THE REVIVING POWER OF COFFEE

Ethiopian legends tell of the shepherd Kaldi,
who on observing his goats dancing about
after eating the red berries of a certain shrub,
discovered the stimulating powers of coffee for
himself. Coffee beans were first eaten whole;
later the berries were made into a wine. Roasting
coffee beans to make a beverage did not come
into practice until some four hundred years after
its first recorded use, but today a hot cup of
coffee is one of the world's favourite drinks.

FRENCH HAZELNUT MOCHA TOWER,

recipe page 122

December

The Heartbreak of Narcissus

Narcissus was a beautiful young man cursed by the goddess Nemesis to suffer unrequited love. He fell in love with his own reflection. Try as he might, he could not embrace his watery love, nor could he leave the sweet apparition whose sensitive face matched his every emotion and, like him, grew pale and wan. Narcissus perished of thirst and on the spot where he died a delicate flower grew, the narcissus – a symbol of love and despair.

December

In Greek myth, the centaur Chiron was
a kind and gifted teacher and the mentor
of many heroes, including the mighty-but-
clumsy Hercules, who accidentally shot
his beloved tutor with a poisoned
arrow, delivering him a
mortal wound. Thereupon
the gods transferred Chiron to
the heavens where he shines as
the archer Sagittarius.

SAGITTARIUS - *Nov 22 - Dec 21*

Sagittarians are optimistic,
honest and good-humoured.
They are prone to restlessness;
they love to travel and readily embrace
new experiences. Naturally intellectual
with a sociable bent, they make
wonderful teachers.

Jane Austen - 1775
English author

17	18
19	20
21	22
23	24

DECEMBER

Turquoise

Turquoise has been treasured for its spiritual
and protective qualities ever since the Aztecs
proclaimed it sacred and reserved it for
the use of the gods. In Tibet, turquoise is worn as
a blessing and protection from evil.
For Native American tribes, the beautiful
blue-green stone unites the spirits of the sea
and the sky and blesses the wearer.

*Calmness of mind is one of the beautiful
jewels of wisdom.*

James Allen

25

26

27

28

29

30

31

Henri Matisse - 1869
French artist

Holly

December

The Sweetness of Dried Grapes

Delicious raisins, sultanas and currants are all different varieties of dried grapes. Ever since crops were cultivated, fruit has been dried to create sweet, preservable food. Sultanas originated from a white, seedless grape from Turkey, and Europeans named them after the feminine form of the Turkish title of sultan. Surprisingly, currants have nothing to do with the currant berry; they are tiny raisins made with a black, seedless grape from Greece.

Overnight Christmas Cake, *see recipe page 124*

MISSISSIPPI MUD CAKE *with* CHOCOLATE GANACHE

PREP	15 minutes
COOK	1½ hours
MAKES	1 x 25cm cake, serves 10-12

Originating from the American South, this dense, moist chocolate cake is as thick and gooey as Mississippi river mud – but much tastier! It makes a spectacular party cake, especially for chocoholics.

INGREDIENTS

375g butter, chopped

600g / 4 cups good quality dark eating chocolate, chopped

2 tbsp dry instant coffee

330g / 1½ cups firmly packed brown sugar

250ml / 1 cup boiling water

4 eggs, beaten

2 tbsp coffee liqueur

185g / 1½ cups plain or cake flour

45g / ⅓ cup self-raising flour

PREHEAT oven to 165°C fan bake. Grease a deep 25cm cake tin and line the base and sides with three layers of baking paper.

PLACE the butter, chocolate, dry coffee, brown sugar and water in a pan and heat until the butter is just melted. Remove from heat and beat in the eggs and coffee liqueur. Sift the dry ingredients and fold into wet mixture with a large flat spoon until just combined.

SPOON the mixture into prepared cake tin and bake for 1½ hours until risen and when a skewer inserted into the centre of the cake comes out clean.

LEAVE cake to cool in tin. Turn out when cold and ice.

PLACE the cream in a saucepan and bring to a simmer. Take off the heat and add the chopped chocolate. Stir until glossy and smooth. Cool to a spreading consistency, about 1 hour. Beat ⅔ of the ganache until creamy and then use 1 cup of this whipped ganache to sandwich the two cakes together.

SPREAD the remaining whipped ganache over top and sides of cake. Warm the remaining ganache to a flowing consistency and drizzle over the top of the cake. Store cake in a sealed container in a cool place for up to 2 weeks or freeze.

MELT dark chocolate to make cake decorations on baking paper. Allow these to set before attaching to the cake with a little ganache.

CHOCOLATE GANACHE ICING

1kg good quality dark eating chocolate, chopped

1 litre / 4 cups cream

MY CELEBRATION RECORD

CATHEDRAL CAKE

PREP   15 minutes, plus overnight standing

COOK   2 hours

MAKES   1 x 23cm cake, serves 10-12

Slicing into this cake is like looking into a stained glass window. Dense with dried fruits and nuts, its rich flavours evoke the lush groves of almonds, cherries and figs of the Ancient Mediterranean. You can use dates in combination with 800g of any other dried fruit.

FRUIT AND NUTS

150g / 1 cup glacé red cherries

120g / 1 cup dried papaya or mango chunks

60g / ½ cup dried pineapple pieces

165g / 1 cup dried figs, quartered

185g / 1 cup prunes, quartered

125g / 1 cup dried cranberries

370g / 2 cups chopped dried pitted dates

185ml / ¾ cup rum, brandy or whiskey

125ml / ½ cup water

240g / 2 cups whole Brazil nuts

230g / 1½ cups whole almonds

BATTER

3 eggs

220g / 1 cup firmly packed brown sugar

1 tsp vanilla essence

1 tsp rum essence or almond essence

155g / 1¼ cups plain or cake flour

1 tbsp cinnamon

1 tsp ground cloves

1 tsp Chinese five spice

½ tsp baking powder

¼ tsp salt

PLACE the fruit, reserving 1 cup dates, in a large mixing bowl with the alcohol. Stand overnight.

PREHEAT oven to 130°C fan bake. Grease and line a 23cm cake tin with baking paper. Place reserved dates in a bowl with water, cover and microwave for 5 minutes, or boil for 5 minutes in a pot. Stir well to break up dates. Add cooked dates and nuts to the soaked fruit and combine evenly with a large spoon.

IN A SEPARATE BOWL, beat eggs, sugar and essences to combine. Add flour, spices, baking powder and salt and mix to a smooth batter. Pour batter over fruit and nuts and mix to combine evenly (there will be very little batter). Spoon the thick mixture into prepared tin, pressing down firmly with the back of a spoon. Bake for two hours or until top of cake feels firm.

STAND for 10 minutes, then turn out. Allow to cool. Wrap the cake with tin foil to prevent it drying out before storing in an airtight container.

ALLOW to cool fully before garnishing. Heat apricot jam in the microwave for 30 seconds or heat in a pot for 1 minute. Brush jam over the cake. Arrange dried fruit and nuts on top. Apply remaining jam over the top to glaze. Use a hot, sharp knife to cut.

OPTIONAL GARNISH

¼ cup apricot jam, melted

mixture of dried fruits and nuts to decorate

MY CELEBRATION RECORD

EASTER SIMNEL CAKE

PREP   20 minutes

COOK   45 minutes

MAKES   1 x 20cm cake, serves 6-8

In the Middle Ages, simnel cakes celebrated Mothering Sunday, when people returned to their "mother church". Now an Easter cake, the balls on the top represent all the apostles of Jesus except Judas.

FILLING

100g butter

185g / 1 cup semolina

250ml / 1 cup water

250g / 1 cup sugar

2 tsp almond essence

BATTER

125g butter

125g / ½ cup sugar

3 eggs

600g / 3¾ cups mixed dried fruit

½ tsp almond essence

125g / 1 cup plain or cake flour

1 tsp baking powder

1 tsp mixed spice

OPTIONAL 60ml / ¼ cup sherry

PREHEAT oven to 160°C fan bake. Grease and line a 20cm cake tin with baking paper.

PREPARE filling mixture first. Melt the butter in a pot with semolina and ¼ of the cup of water, stirring to make a paste. Add remaining water, sugar and essence and stir over low heat until mixture has thickened and is smooth, 2 minutes. Allow to cool.

TO MAKE cake batter, beat butter and sugar together until light and creamy. Beat in eggs; mix in fruit and essence, then fold in combined dry ingredients until evenly mixed. Spread half of the cake batter in the tin, and then spread over half the semolina mixture. Cover with the remaining cake batter, smoothing the surface out evenly. Chill the remaining semolina mixture.

BAKE for 40-45 minutes until cake is set and golden. Spoon sherry over top while cake is hot. Leave cake in the tin to cool then turn out onto a serving plate.

To MAKE icing, beat all ingredients together until smooth and creamy. Ice cake. Decorate cake by dividing the chilled semolina mixture into 11 pieces; roll into balls and place evenly around the cake top. Cake will keep in a sealed container in the fridge for up to a week.

LEMON ICING

50g butter, melted

250g / 2 cups icing sugar

zest of 1 lemon

3 tbsp lemon juice

MY CELEBRATION RECORD

APRICOT & ALMOND LAYERED WEDDING CAKE
with WHITE CHOCOLATE ICING

PREP   20 minutes

COOK   40-45 minutes

MAKES   1 x 4-tiered 25cm cake, serves up to 20

Don't try to make this divine cake without an electric beater. A simple Génoise sponge, it needs a good beating at the start to get the egg and sugar mixture the right consistency. The sponge and purée can be made ahead of time; you can freeze the sponge, it's easier to slice when frozen. Once iced, the cake will keep for a week in a cool place.

SPONGE

100g / 1 cup ground almonds or hazelnuts

6 eggs

315g / 1¼ cups sugar

finely grated zest of 1 orange

¼ tsp almond essence

155g / 1¼ cups plain or cake flour

pinch salt

50g butter, melted

FILLING

300g / 2⅛ cups dried apricots

250g / 1 cup sugar

875ml / 3½ cups water

PREHEAT oven to 160°C fan bake. Toast ground almonds or hazelnuts on an oven tray, 10 minutes. Remove and allow to cool. Increase oven temperature to 170°C. Grease and line a 25cm cake tin with baking paper.

PLACE eggs and sugar in mixer, using the whisk, beat on high until thick, pale and ribbony, about 10 minutes. Beat in orange rind and almond essence. Sift over half the flour, add salt; gently fold into mixture with a large, flat spoon. Sift over remaining flour and fold in gently. Follow with ground almonds and butter. Spoon mixture into tin and gently spread out evenly. Bake in the middle of the oven for 40-45 minutes until edges start to come away from the sides and cake is set in the centre. Remove from oven and cool in tin.

WHILE cake cooks, prepare filling. Heat apricots, sugar and water in a pot, stirring over medium heat until sugar dissolves. Simmer until soft, about 15-20 minutes, or microwave in a covered container, 10 minutes. Cool and purée until smooth; the mixture should be jam-like in consistency. Add a little more water if needed.

USING a sharp bread knife carefully slice cake into 4 layers. Spread each layer with purée and reassemble cake from bottom up. Brush top and sides of the whole cake with a thin coating of purée. Chill for at least ½ hour before icing.

TO ICE, cover and microwave white chocolate and cream until just melted, stirring every 30 seconds, or heat in a pot, stirring regularly until smooth. Remove from heat; add icing sugar, stirring until smooth. Brush a thin layer of icing all over the cake. Cool until chocolate sets, then repeat until cake is fully covered. Use a hot, sharp knife to cut.

MELT white chocolate to make cake decorations on baking paper. Allow these to set before attaching to the cake with a little softened chocolate.

ICING

800g white chocolate, chopped

500ml / 2 cups cream

500g / 4 cups icing sugar

OPTIONAL

200g white chocolate for garnish

MY CELEBRATION RECORD

White Chocolate & Raspberry Bombe Alaska

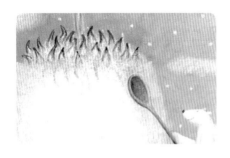

PREP	15 minutes, plus at least 6 hours freezing
COOK	2-3 minutes
MAKES	10 small bombes or 1 large bombe, serves 10

Whoever thought of encasing ice cream and sponge in toasted meringue was a gastronomic genius. The name refers to the version by Chef Charles Ranhofer celebrating the 1876 American purchase of Alaska.

INGREDIENTS

2 litres / 8 cups premium white chocolate and raspberry ice cream (or a flavour of your choice)

2 x 20cm squares or rounds of chocolate sponge cake

3 tbsp raspberry jam

MERINGUE TOPPING

330g / 1½ cup caster sugar

80ml / ⅓ cup water

5 egg whites, at room temperature

¼ tsp cream of tartar

LINE 10 dessert cups or ramekins with plastic wrap, allowing the wrap to overhang on all sides. Cut sponge to fit the top of the moulds. Allow ice cream to soften slightly at room temperature, or if frozen, heat for 30 seconds in microwave on low; spoon into the moulds and press down firmly with a spoon. Spread a teaspoon of jam on one side of the sponge tops and invert them jam-side down over the ice cream. Press firmly to stick. Cover and freeze for at least 6 hours or up to a week.

IN A SMALL POT over low heat, combine sugar and water. Do not stir. Swirl the pot over the burner to dissolve the sugar completely. Use a wet pastry brush to wash down the inside walls of the pot with a little cold water to stop the sugar mixture crystallizing. If this happens you will need to start this process again.

INCREASE the heat and boil to a "soft ball" stage (115°C or 240°F on a candy thermometer). To check, drop a small spoonful into cold water;

the mixture should be firm enough to shape into a soft ball.

IN A CLEAN BOWL, whip the egg whites with an electric mixer on low speed until foamy. Add cream of tartar, increase speed to medium and beat until soft peaks form, about 5 minutes. With the mixer running, pour the boiling hot sugar syrup in a thin stream over the egg whites. Beat until stiff and glossy, about 5 minutes.

REMOVE ice cream moulds from the freezer and invert sponge-side down onto an ovenproof tray that will fit in the freezer. Remove plastic wrap and pipe or spread meringue mixture over the ice cream-sponge, covering sides and tops fully. Refreeze until ready to serve (bombes can be kept in the freezer for several days).

PREHEAT oven to 220°C fan bake. Place tray directly from freezer into the hot oven and cook for 2-3 minutes until bombes are light golden-brown. Transfer quickly to plates and serve immediately.

MY CELEBRATION RECORD

LEMON & VANILLA BUTTERFLY CUPCAKES

PREP   10 minutes

COOK   20-25 minutes

MAKES   8 cupcakes

These pretty cakes will be a hit at any children's party – if the adults don't eat them first. Cupcakes are so versatile: change out the flavours, ice in different colours or even stack them to form one large cake.

INGREDIENTS

100g butter

165g / ¾ cup caster sugar

1 tbsp finely grated lemon zest

2 eggs

125g/ 1 cup plain or cake flour

2 tsp baking powder

105ml / 7 tbsp lemon juice, warmed

LEMON FROSTING

250g cream cheese

100g butter, softened

4 cups / 500g icing sugar

1 tsp finely grated lemon zest

PREHEAT oven to 160°C fan bake. Arrange 8 paper cupcake cases in a medium muffin tray. Beat butter, sugar and lemon rind until pale and creamy. Beat in eggs one at a time. Sift flour and baking powder together. Fold the dry ingredients and lemon juice alternately into creamed mixture with a large flat spoon until a smooth batter is formed. Do not over mix.

DIVIDE mixture between paper cases (about 4 tbsp of mixture per case). Bake for 20-25 minutes until risen and light golden. Cool before icing.

TO MAKE frosting, beat cream cheese and butter until smooth. Gradually beat in icing sugar and lemon rind until mixture is pale and creamy, at least 5 minutes. Pour into a piping bag to ice.

CUT small circles out of the top of each cupcake. Pipe frosting generously into the holes. Slice the circles in half and place as "wings" on top of the cakes, press lightly into the frosting.

DUST with icing sugar and decorate to look like butterflies; use a soft jelly sweet for the body of the butterfly and two pieces of thin liquorice rope for the antennae.

MY CELEBRATION RECORD

GINGER CAKE *with* CARAMEL ICING

PREP   10 minutes

COOK   45 minutes

SERVES   1 x 20cm cake, serves 6-8

A spicy, moist cake with rich icing, this is a wonderful cake for a special afternoon tea. It's an old fashioned cake, but one which both young and old will enjoy. Perfect for making ahead of time, it keeps well in an airtight container or can be frozen and iced on thawing. The yoghurt or buttermilk provides acidity, which makes the mixture very tender.

INGREDIENTS

100g butter, softened

125g / ½ cup sugar

170g / ½ cup treacle

45g / ¼ cup finely chopped crystallized ginger

2 eggs, at room temperature

185g / 1½ cups plain or cake flour

1 tsp baking soda

4 tsp ground ginger

1 tsp each mixed spice and cinnamon

125ml / ½ cup natural yogurt or buttermilk

PREHEAT oven to 165°C fan bake. Grease and line a 20cm cake tin with baking paper.

IN A LARGE MIXING BOWL, beat together the butter and sugar until pale and creamy. Add treacle and ginger; continue beating. Add eggs one at a time, beating well after each addition.

SIFT dry ingredients together and add to the wet mixture alternately with the yogurt or buttermilk, mixing until smooth. Pour into prepared tin and smooth the surface out evenly. Bake for 45 minutes until golden and springy to the touch. Stand for 10 minutes before turning out. Cool fully before icing.

TO MAKE icing, cream butter, sugar and golden syrup until light and fluffy. Add icing sugar and milk, stirring until smooth. Spread icing over cooled cake. Garnish with sliced crystallized ginger.

CARAMEL ICING

125g unsalted butter

220g / 1 cup brown sugar

4 tsp golden syrup

2 tsp milk

190g / 1½ cups icing sugar

4 tbsp crystallized ginger, sliced

MY CELEBRATION RECORD

GREEK CITRUS CAKE

PREP   15 minutes

COOK   30-35 minutes

MAKES   1 x 23cm cake, serves 10-12

This is a delicate, sophisticated cake, ideal for more formal occasions, or for those who don't like icing. The delicious, tangy syrup and the use of semolina and ground almonds give it a fine, moist texture. It will keep in a cool place for over a week. The syrup is also useful to have on hand as a garnish for fresh fruit salads.

INGREDIENTS

90g / ¾ cup self-raising flour

1 tsp baking powder

90g / ½ cup semolina

100g / 1 cup ground almonds

125g unsalted butter

220g / 1 cup caster sugar

finely grated zest of 1 lemon and

½ an orange

1 tsp natural vanilla essence

3 eggs, at room temperature

60ml / ¼ cup lemon juice

12-16 whole peeled almonds,

to garnish

PREHEAT oven to 170°C fan bake. Grease and line a 23cm spring-form cake tin with baking paper.

IN A BOWL, sift together flour and baking powder; add semolina and ground almonds. In another mixing bowl beat butter and sugar together until light and creamy. Beat in zests and vanilla. Add eggs one at a time, beating well after each addition.

STIR in half the flour mixture then the lemon juice. Gently stir in the remaining flour mixture until evenly combined. Pour mixture into prepared tin and decorate with almonds. Bake for 30-35 minutes until a skewer inserted in the centre comes out clean and the top is springy to the touch.

To MAKE syrup, place all ingredients in a pot and bring to a simmer, stirring to dissolve sugar. Boil until syrupy, about 10 minutes. Brush citrus syrup over hot cake. Serve cake with crème fraîche or whipped cream on the side.

CITRUS SYRUP

180ml / ¾ cup mix of orange and lemon juice

125g / ½ cup sugar

peeled rind of 1 lemon (no pith), sliced into very thin strips

2 cardamom pods or 1 whole star anise

1 tsp vanilla essence

MY CELEBRATION RECORD

HUMMINGBIRD CAKE

PREP   20 minutes

COOK   55-60 minutes

MAKES   1 x 25cm cake, serves 10-12

Impress your family and friends with this beautiful humdinger of a cake. Packed full of delicious tropical fruit flavours, it will please all tastes and even though it's big enough for a crowd, it won't last! This cake will keep in a sealed container in a cool place for several days or in the fridge for over a week, or can be iced and frozen for a complete no-fuss delivery.

INGREDIENTS

250g butter, softened

375g / 1½ cups sugar

4 eggs

2 tsp natural vanilla essence

3 very ripe bananas, peeled and mashed (about 2 cups)

430g can / 2⅓ cups crushed pineapple, well-drained

60g / ½ cup desiccated coconut

2 tbsp passionfruit pulp or syrup

2 tsp baking soda

125ml / ½ cup hot milk

375g / 3 cups plain or cake flour

3 tsp baking powder

PREHEAT oven to 160°C fan bake. Grease and line a 25cm round cake tin with baking paper.

BEAT butter and sugar until light and creamy. Beat in eggs and vanilla, stir in bananas, pineapple, coconut and passionfruit. Dissolve baking soda in hot milk, cool slightly and add to mixture. Sift over flour and baking powder and fold in to form a smooth batter.

SPOON mixture into prepared tin and smooth the surface out evenly.

BAKE for 55-60 minutes or until a skewer inserted in the centre comes out clean and the top is springy to the touch.

REMOVE from oven and cool in baking tin. Remove from tin and ice when thoroughly cooled.

To MAKE icing, beat cream cheese and butter until smooth and creamy. Mix in other ingredients, whisking until icing is smooth. Spread over cake, top and sides. If using, drizzle over passionfruit and decorate with pineapple pieces.

CREAM CHEESE ICING

185g cream cheese

75g butter, softened

750g / 6 cups icing sugar

1 tsp vanilla essence

finely grated zest of 1 lemon

3 tbsp lemon juice

OPTIONAL

2 tbsp passionfruit pulp or syrup and crystallized pineapple to garnish

MY CELEBRATION RECORD

ANGEL RASPBERRY LAYER CAKE

PREP   10 minutes, plus 15 minutes beating

COOK   45-50 minutes

MAKES   1 x 20cm 3-tiered sponge, serves 8-10

So airy and so delicious, this charming cake must be the food of angels. The simple sponge base is light enough to fill with whipped cream and fresh berries, yet sturdy enough to transport to a party.

SPONGE

6 eggs, at room temperature

220g / 1 cup caster sugar

155g / 1¼ cups plain or cake flour

60g / ½ cup cornflour

45g butter, melted and cooled

4 tbsp raspberry jam

BERRY CREAM

250g / 2 cups raspberries or mixed berries (fresh or thawed frozen)

60g / ½ cup icing sugar

1 tbsp kirsch or orange juice

250ml / 1 cup cream, chilled

PREHEAT oven to 170°C fan bake. Grease and line a 20cm cake tin with baking paper to cover the base and form a 10cm-high collar (the paper will extend above the rim of the tin).

USING an electric mixer beat eggs and sugar at full speed until mixture is very thick, pale and creamy, about 15-20 minutes. Sift the flours together and fold gently into egg mixture until evenly combined. Do not over mix. Gently fold in melted butter until mixture is evenly incorporated.

POUR mixture into prepared tin, spread out evenly and bake for 45-50 minutes until golden and a skewer inserted in the centre comes out clean. Remove from oven and turn tin upside down on a cake rack. Remove sponge from tin while still warm. To store, seal in plastic wrap when cooled. Sponge will keep fresh for several days or can be frozen.

WHILE the cake cools prepare the berry coulis. Purée berries with icing sugar and kirsch or orange juice; strain through a sieve to remove pips.

IN A SEPARATE BOWL whip the chilled cream to soft peaks.

WHEN ready to assemble, fold all but 2 tbsp of the berry coulis into the whipped cream.

USE a serrated knife to cut cooled sponge horizontally into three layers. Spread bottom layer of sponge with 2 tbsp jam, ½ the berry cream and a ⅓ of the berries. Place the next layer of cake on top and spread with remaining jam, berry cream and ⅓ of the berries. Place last round of sponge on top, dust with icing sugar and decorate with remaining berries and reserved berry coulis.

THE ASSEMBLED CAKE needs to be kept in a cool place and served within 3-4 hours.

GARNISH

300-400g / about 3 cups fresh berries

MY CELEBRATION RECORD

121

FRENCH HAZELNUT MOCHA TOWER

PREP   15 minutes, plus at least 4 hours chilling

COOK   12 minutes

MAKES   1 x 18cm, 4-tiered cake, serves 6-8

Bring a lovely romantic anniversary dinner to a truly impressive close with this rich coffee and chocolate treat. Either buy a sponge for quick assembly or make this easy recipe.

CHOCOLATE SPONGE

3 eggs, separated

185g / ¾ cup sugar

80g / ⅔ cup cornflour

1½ tbsp plain flour

1½ tsp baking powder

2 tbsp cocoa, sifted

COFFEE SYRUP

125ml / ½ cup strong coffee, cooled

60ml / ¼ cup coffee liqueur or rum

PREHEAT oven to 180°C fan bake. Grease and line 2 x 18cm round cake tins with baking paper. Beat egg whites to soft peaks in a large clean bowl then beat in sugar until dissolved, about 2 minutes. Beat in yolks. Sift dry ingredients and fold into mixture gently with a large, flat spoon. Divide mixture into prepared cake tins, smoothing tops evenly.

BAKE for 12 minutes until risen and sponges bounce back when gently pressed. Cool for 5 minutes before removing from tins.

LINE an 18cm a spring-form cake tin with plastic wrap, allowing the wrap to overhang on all sides.

PREPARE Cream Cheese Filling (see right).

CUT each sponge in half horizontally. Place one round of sponge to cover the base of the prepared tin. Combine coffee and liqueur. Brush 3 tbsp of this mixture over the sponge in tin and spoon ⅓ of the cream cheese filling over the top. Repeat these steps with 2 more sponge rounds. For the top sponge round, brush with the remaining coffee mixture.

COVER and chill for at least 4 hours or up to 24 hours before serving. Dust with cocoa and sprinkle with hazelnuts just before serving. This cake can be frozen and defrosted (about 2 hours) before serving.

To Prepare Cream Cheese Filling:
USING an electric beater, beat icing sugar, cream cheese, lemon juice and zest, vanilla and ground cloves until smooth.

Cream Cheese Filling

60g / ½ cup icing sugar

400g reduced fat cream cheese

2 tsp lemon juice

finely grated zest of ½ a lemon

1 tsp vanilla essence

½ tsp ground cloves

Garnish

1 tbsp cocoa, sieved

2 tbsp chopped hazelnuts

My Celebration Record

OVERNIGHT CHRISTMAS CAKE

PREP   20 minutes

COOK   12 hours

SERVES   1 x 25cm cake, serves 20

This recipe celebrates the power of tradition in flavours that we come back to year after year. Every family has their own version or variation, which travels from friend to friend and generation to generation. This cake makes a wonderful Christmas gift, and can be cooked as one big cake, or baked in four small tins.

INGREDIENTS

500g butter

500g / 2 cups sugar

10 eggs

2 tbsp brandy or sherry

560g / 4½ cups plain or cake flour

½ tsp baking powder

½ tsp salt

1.45kg mixed dried fruit, e.g currants, sultanas, raisins and dates

150g / 1 cup mixed peel

150g / 1 cup glacé cherries

300g / 2 cups mixed nuts, eg almond and Brazil

120ml (1 sherry glass) sherry to pour over cake

PREHEAT oven to 100°C (do not use fan bake as it will dry this cake out). Grease and line a 25cm square cake tin with three layers of baking paper.

BEAT together butter and sugar until light and creamy, add eggs and brandy or sherry and mix well. Sift flour and baking powder and add salt.

MIX dried fruit and nuts with dry ingredients before adding to the egg mixture. Use a large wooden spoon or clean hands to combine evenly.

SPOON mixture into prepared tin, pressing it in firmly. Cook overnight, 12 hours. Remove from oven and immediately pour sherry over the top.

KEEP the cake in the tin until absolutely cold. Cake keeps for weeks if covered and stored in airtight container in a cool place. The icing will harden and help to preserve the cake.

To ice and decorate the cake:

TRIM the top of the cake to create a flat surface. Invert the cake flat side down. Brush cake with a little apricot jam over all sides – this will prevent the marzipan from slipping. Sprinkle work surface with a little icing sugar, knead and roll out marzipan to a size that will cover base and sides of cake completely. Lay marzipan over cake carefully, trimming any excess. Roll out white icing to the same size and cover base and sides completely, trimming any excess. Leave the icing to harden overnight. This can be done up to three weeks before the cake is eaten.

ONCE the icing has hardened, the royal icing can be applied. Gently beat egg white until slightly airy. Add icing sugar and beat, 10 minutes. Place mixture in piping bag; pipe Christmas tree shapes or other patterns directly onto the cake. You can also ice shapes onto a piece of baking paper and when set, carefully transfer to the cake, using a little wet icing to secure. Decorate with silver cachous balls as desired.

ICING

½ cup apricot jam, heated and strained

750g commercial almond / marzipan icing

750g commercial white icing / fondant

ROYAL ICING

1 egg white

250g / 2 cups icing sugar

silver cachous balls to garnish

MY CELEBRATION RECORD

Your Better Baking Guide

Baking is a reasonably precise chemistry and you need to measure the ingredients carefully. Stick to one form of measure, be it cups or weights, as they are not interchangeable. If something does go wrong, don't lose heart. A dusting of icing sugar is great redeemer for anything burnt or misshapen, and if your cake sinks, just turn it upside down or fill the hole with icing – someone is bound to be pleased with the extra dose of sugar.

Oven Heat

The recipes in this book were tested in a fan bake oven. If using a non-fan bake oven you may need to add about 10% to the cooking time or increase the heat by 5-10°C. All ovens cook differently. For this reason, and because ingredients differ in moisture content and liquid absorption etc, you need to use your judgement and treat the cooking times as a guide. Once you evaluate how your oven sits in relation to the recipes in this book you will be able to judge the times accordingly. Remember to preheat your oven before you start cooking.

Flour Type

The term high-grade does not indicate better quality flour; it refers to the amount of protein in the flour and consequently the level of gluten it produces. High-grade flour produces tough cakes with ugly peaked tops – this can also result from over mixing the cake batter. With the exception of fruit cakes, which require high-protein flour, this book specifics the use of plain or cake flour to ensure light, well-shaped cakes.

Shortcuts

With such good commercial baked products, sauces and fillings now available you can easily assemble a fantastic cake without having to start from scratch. Take a commercial sponge and fill it with fresh, sliced strawberries and whipped cream, or whip mascarpone with a little icing sugar and vanilla, then layer into the sponge with raspberry jam or your favourite syrup, a dusting of icing sugar and your cake looks as good as something home-made. Don't feel guilty about taking shortcuts – it's all about creating a sense of celebration and fun.

Preparing & Caring for Cake Tins

If you grease a cake tin with a little spray oil or softened butter, when you come to line it with baking paper or parchment, the paper will stick inside the tin easily. It often helps to soak the used tin in hot water and detergent before cleaning. Once clean, rinse thoroughly and dry in the cooling oven. This will ensure your tins remain rust free.

TESTING FOR DONENESS

When your kitchen starts to smell delicious, you know your cake is probably ready. Until you get to know your own oven, it is a good idea to check on your cake 5-10 minutes before the specified cooking time. Confirm that a cake is ready with one of two simple tests: gently touch the top of the cake, it should bounce back; or, plunge a thin skewer into the middle of the cake, if it comes out clean, the cake is ready.

ICING & FILLINGS

Cakes need to be fully cooled before they are iced. Sponge cakes, which have a very fragile crust, can easily tear when iced. Either spread the sponge with a little melted jam before icing, or freeze and ice while still frozen. If you like a cake but not the specified icing or filling, create your own special recipe match with a different icing or topping. Ginger Cake with Caramel Icing is delicious topped with Lemon Frosting from the Lemon and Vanilla Butterfly Cupcakes.

STORING & FREEZING CAKES

Make sure your cake is fully cooled before storing in an airtight container or it could go mouldy. Moist cakes, such as the Hummingbird Cake, are best stored in the fridge if keeping for more than 2-3 days. Most cakes are best eaten fresh, with the exception of fruit cakes, which improve with age. Sponges go stale quickly, but they freeze well. If you are not planning to eat a sponge within 1-2 days, freeze in an airtight container. If freezing, ice cakes while frozen and allow 2-3 hours at room temperature to thaw. Any of the cream cheese based icing can be frozen, so you can even freeze a whole iced cake if desired.

Visit the Annabel Langbein website, www.annabel-langbein.com, for more details on icing and decorating cakes, as well as photographs of the finished cakes in this book. You will also find online seasonal collections of Annabel's recipes, her instructional cooking videos, plus simple and enjoyable hints on how eat well and live well.

Better Baking Hints

Measures Used in This Book

1 cup = 250ml

1 tbsp (tablespoon) = 15ml

1 tsp (teaspoon) = 5ml

Sifting

Passing dry ingredients through a fine sieve removes lumps and ensures a lighter mixture. Sponges benefit from sifting, but it is not necessary for dense fruit cakes.

Beating & Creaming

Beating butter and sugar together until light and creamy is a process known as "creaming". It incorporates extra air into the batter and helps to create extra volume .

Folding

Adding dry ingredients is usually the last step in making a cake batter. To retain a light mixture, it's important not to over mix the batter. Use a large flat spoon and big scooping movements to gently fold the dry ingredients into the wet mixture until just combined. If the recipe calls for the dry ingredients to be added alternately with a liquid, this will ensure that the batter does not become either too wet or too dry during mixing.

Whipping

Cream needs to be chilled before it is whipped, it should then should be covered and refrigerated if not using at once. Cream will become grainy if it gets too warm.

When beating egg whites, make sure the bowl and the beater are clean and that there is no egg yolk whatsoever in the mixture, as this or any other fat will prevent the whites from aerating fully.

When soft or firm peaks are required in cream or egg whites, lift the beater away from the mixture and check the consistency. Soft peaks have a collapsing top while stiff peaks hold their shape firmly.

Melting

Butter can be melted in a pot or a microwave, cover to prevent splattering and watch it does not burn. Take care with chocolate, which if overheated will "seize" in an irretrievable fashion. Melt chocolate in a double boiler, or heat in the microwave in bursts of 30-60 seconds, stirring well between each instance until smooth and glossy.